D0734898

NEAL BOORTZ

The Commencement Speech

You Need To Hear

NEAL BOORTZ

The

Commencement

Speech

You

Need

To

Hear

LONGSTREET PRESS
Atlanta, GA

Published by LONGSTREET PRESS, INC.,
a subsidiary of Cox Newspapers,
a subsidiary of Cox Enterprises, Inc.
2140 Newmarket Parkway
Suite 122
Marietta, Georgia 30067

Printed in the United States of America

1st printing, 1997

Library of Congress Catalog Number: 97-71936

ISBN: 1-56352-434-1

Electronic film prep by OGI, Forest Park, GA
Cover/book design by Graham & Co. Graphics, Inc.

DEDICATION

To my wife, Donna.
My Soulmate and best friend;
and to our daughter, Laura,
a source of love, joy and pride.
The rest of you should be so lucky.

OK. SO WHO IS THIS
Neal Boortz Guy?

In the fall of 1969 Neal Boortz, quickly tiring of his jobs as a carpet installer and executive search consultant, decided a new career path was in order. He was going nowhere and his knees were getting sore.

After hearing that WRNG (Ring Radio)'s most controversial talk show host had killed himself (No, really. A gun to the head. Bang! Thud! Dirt nap.), Boortz called the Atlanta station and offered his services as the new controversial talk show host.

It was a classic case of right place / right time. Boortz was hired to do some fill-in work, and two weeks later he found himself the permanent host of "The Neal Boortz Show." He's been at it, enraging Atlanta, ever since.

Today, twenty-eight years after starting on Ring Radio, Boortz hosts Atlanta's No. 1 radio show on News Talk 750 WSB in Atlanta.

In 1996 Boortz was recognized by the Georgia Association of Broadcasters as Georgia's No. 1 major market radio personality, and *Talker's Magazine* named him "America's Best Male Talk Show Host."

These accolades earned Boortz a small bonus from WSB, which he exhausted in buying an old IBM Selectric typewriter on which "The Neal Boortz Commencement Speech" was written.

INTRODUCTION

You hold in your hand the next step in your education. If you're about to graduate from college, consider this as the commencement speech you need to hear, instead of the garbage you're likely to hear. If you're a relatively recent graduate, consider this as continuing education. And if you're a weathered graduate, consider this as yet another valuable lesson in that proverbial School of Hard Knocks.

Either way, it's a strong dose of anti-liberal venom, designed to help you recover from a long assault on your rational immune system.

In college, you spent four years or so in the grip of America's Liberal Academia. Day after day you were subjected to a seemingly endless procession of liberal college professors who you knew couldn't possibly find meaningful employment in the private sector. They programmed you with the big-government, forced-compassion ideology they acquired in the '60s, and they tried to convince you that anyone who did not agree with them was either evil, insensitive, ignorant, hate-filled, or all of the above.

So, what did you finally get out of college? Well, in addition to a sprinkling of basic knowledge that might, with a little bit of luck, come in handy in your chosen field, you spent four years learning (just for starters) that:

1. It is better to "feel" and to "care" than to "think" and to "reason."
2. Those who succeed in life do so through "luck."
3. Those who fail in life do so because they are the "less fortunate."
4. One person's failure constitutes a lien on another person's hard work and success.
5. Income is distributed, not earned.
6. When anything bad ever happens to any member of an officially recognized minority group, it is because of either racism or sexism.
7. The Left is good, and the Right is evil.

8. Private businesses are the causes of the problems of society, and more government is the only solution.

9. We really have no need for a military anymore, except to deliver flour and corn dogs to refugees.

10. Taxes in the United States are too low, and the rich certainly don't pay their "fair share."

11. Your parents are hopeless reactionary tools of the corporate structure.

12. Anyone who has more than you got it through greed.

13. Bill Clinton is actually to be admired.

To make matters worse, you probably heard (or will hear) more of the same nonsense during your graduation ceremonies!

For years I have lamented the fact that I have never been invited to deliver a commencement address at a college or university. Finally, after learning that even Kermit the Frog was getting invitations, I decided I had had enough. On June 6, 1996, I delivered my own commencement speech to my alert and attentive listeners on News Talk 750 WSB in Atlanta.

After "The Commencement Speech" was delivered on my radio show, I started fielding hundreds of requests for tapes or transcripts. A recording of the speech became available on a "Best of Boortz '96" compact disc in December 1996. The first printing of the CD sold out in less than 24 hours. The second printing lasted only a few days longer.

Now, for the first time, "The Commencement Speech" is available in book form. It is followed here by a series of embellishments that I call "Debugging the New Graduate." The commencement address is like an introductory survey course; the debugging tips are like graduate courses. If I repeat myself, it is intentional; reversing four years of brainwashing is not easy.

Please be aware that prolonged exposure to unchallenged liberalism can rot your mind, stain your teeth, and make your breath smell foul, and that's not even getting into the incontinence thing. Hurry! Start reading now. There's no time to lose!

SPECIAL NOTE TO THE READER
ON POLITICAL CORRECTNESS

There will be no attempt whatsoever in either "The Commencement Speech" or in "Debugging the New Graduate" at political correctness. I will, for instance, follow the time-honored custom of using "he" and "his" in reference to entities and persons of undetermined gender. I will not plug in the occasional "she" or "hers" to placate someone's tender sensibilities. You're in the real world now, not the protected halls of academia. Time to start getting used to it.

THE NEAL BOORTZ
Commencement Speech

We operate on the assumption at the beginning of this stirring address that a gracious introduction of Mr. Boortz has been delivered by a very junior member of the faculty who owed a lot of people a lot of favors. As Boortz takes to the podium, one or two people actually clap!

Thank you so much for that most gracious introduction. Nice robe.

I am honored by the invitation to address you on this august occasion. It's about time. Be warned, however, that I am not here to impress you; you'll have enough smoke blown at you today. And you can bet your tassels I'm not here to impress the faculty and administration.

After I say what I came to say, there will be precious little chance I will be invited back here to deliver another address. Not here, not anywhere. In short order, you will know why.

You may not like much of what I have to say, and that's fine. You will remember it, though. Especially after about 10 years out there in the real world. This, it goes without saying, does not apply to those of you who will seek your careers and your fortunes as government employees.

This gowned gaggle behind me is your faculty. You've heard the old saying that those who can — *do*. Those who can't — *teach*. That sounds deliciously insensitive. But there is often raw truth in insensitivity, just as you often find feel-good falsehoods and lies in compassion. Say good-bye to your faculty now, because you are getting ready to go out there and do. These folks behind me are going to stay right here and teach.

By the way, just because you are leaving this place with a diploma doesn't mean the learning is over. When an FAA flight examiner handed me my private pilot's license many years ago, he said, "Here, this is your ticket to learn." The same can be said for your diploma. Believe me, the learning has just begun. You ain't seen nuthin' yet.

Now, I realize that most of you consider yourselves Liberals. In fact, you are probably very proud of your liberal views. You care so much. You feel so much. You want to help so much. After all, you are such a compassionate and caring person. Hey, that's fine! Now, at this age, is as good a time as any to be a Liberal; as good a time as any to know absolutely everything.

You have plenty of time, starting tomorrow, for the truth to set in.

Over the next few years, as you begin to feel the cold breath of reality down your neck, things will change. You will change. If not you, certainly that person next to you.

So here are the first assignments for your initial class in reality: Pay attention to the news, read newspapers, and listen to the words and phrases that proud Liberals use to promote their causes; then compare these to the words and phrases you hear from those evil, heartless, greedy Conservatives.

From the Left you will hear "I feel." From the Right you will hear "I think." From the Liberals you will hear references to groups — The Blacks, The Poor, The Rich, The Disadvantaged, The Less Fortunate. From the Right you will hear references to individuals. On the Left we hear talk of group rights; on the Right, individual rights.

That about sums it up, really: Liberals feel. Liberals care.

They are pack animals whose identity is tied up in group dynamics. Conservatives think. And, setting aside the theocracy crowd, their identity is centered on the individual.

Liberals feel that the masses, their favored groups, have enforceable rights to the property and services of productive individuals. Conservatives (and Libertarians, myself among them, I might add) think that individuals have the right to protect their lives and their property from the plunder of the masses.

In college you developed a group identity — Go Panthers! Go Warthogs! Go Tri-Delt, or Go whatever Greek alphabet soup you have been simmering in.

These diplomas, though, have your individual names on them. Not your school mascot, not the name of your fraternity or sorority, but your name. Your individual identity starts now. You're on your own.

If, by the time you reach the age of 30, you do not consider yourself to be a Libertarian or a Conservative, rush right back here as quickly as you can and apply for a faculty position. These people will welcome you with open arms. They will welcome you, that is, so long as you haven't developed an individual identity. You will have to be willing to sign on to the group mentality once again.

Now, I'm not talking in the abstract. I've been there. I've done that. I was one of you. During my college years at Texas A&M, I was a lot further to the left than you are now. I joined the Students for a Democratic Society . . . carried signs . . . occupied the university president's house (well, his front porch anyway). I was *cool*. I was *happening*. I was *aware*. I *cared*. I was *tuned* in. I felt. I *obsessed*. I *followed*. I was a *complete waste*. I did everything but *think*!

What happened, you ask? I got a job! Thinking about it now, maybe I should say we got a job. You see, after I got out of college I found out that I had a lifelong partner that was intent on sharing in every productive thing I did. That partner was, in some ways, an agent. An agent representing a strange and diverse group of people.

An agent for every teenager with an illegitimate child

An agent for a research scientist who wanted to make some cash answering the age-old question of why monkeys grind their teeth.

An agent for some poor demented slob who considered herself to be a meaningful and talented artist . . . but who somehow couldn't manage to sell anything on the open market.

An agent for every person with limited, if any, job skills . . . but who wanted a job at City Hall.

An agent for tin-horn dictators in fancy military uniforms.

An agent for multi-million-dollar companies who wanted someone else to pay for their overseas advertising.

An agent for everybody who wanted to use the unimaginable power this agent has for their personal enrichment and benefit.

That agent is our wonderful, caring, compassionate, oppressive government.

I was petrified at the unimaginable power this agent has. Power that I didn't have. A power that no individual has, or will have. This agent has the legal power to use force. The power to use a gun to accomplish its goals.

I did not necessarily choose this partner in my work life and personal life. The government just walked up, introduced itself rather gruffly, handed me a few forms to fill out, and moved right on in. It slept anywhere it wanted to.

And let me tell you, this agent is not cheap. It takes about 40% of everything I earn. Actually, the way this agent looks at it, it takes 100% of everything I earn and then lets me have about 60% of it back. That 60% is carried as an "expenditure" on my agent's books.

I can't fire this agent, and I can't lower his commission on my work. He has that power, not me.

Be clear on this: It is not wrong to distrust government. It is not wrong to fear government. In certain cases it is not even wrong to despise government. In fact, it may well be praiseworthy. A praiseworthy American tradition.

Government is inherently evil. There's no question it's a necessary evil. After all, we do need some structure to settle disputes between us and to defend against foreign and domestic aggressors. But, like some drugs that in the proper dosage can save your life, an overdose of government can be fatal.

Let's address a few things that have been crammed into your minds at this university. There are some ideas you need to expunge as soon as possible. These ideas may work well in academic environment, but they fail miserably out there in the real world.

We'll talk first about *diversity*. Diversity is a new favorite buzz word of the Left and of academia. You probably spotted one of your professors swooning or breathing heavy when I said the word.

Diversity! *Diversity*! Look at your faculty! The ecstasy on their faces! *Diversity*! I'd better stop. This could get messy.

You have been taught that the real value of any group of people — be it a social group, an employee group, a management group, whatever — is based on diversity. This is a favorite liberal ideal because diversity is based not on an individual's abilities or character, but on a person's identity and status as a member of a group. There we go with that left-wing group dynamics thing again. With diversity the group identification — be it racial, gender based, or some other minority status — means more than the individual's qualifications.

Well, you are about to move from this atmosphere where diversity (whatever that *really* is) counts, to a workplace and a culture where individual achievement and excellence counts. No matter what these mental zombies behind me have taught you for the last four years, you are about to learn that diversity is absolutely no replacement for excellence, ability, and individual hard work.

Next, let's address this thing you seem to have about "rights." We have witnessed an obscene explosion of so-called "rights" in the last few decades, mostly emanating from college campuses.

You know the mantra: You have the *right* to a job. The *right* to a place to live. The *right* to a living wage. The *right* to health care. The *right* to an education. You probably even have your own pet right — the right to a Beemer, for instance, or the right to have someone else provide for that child you plan on downloading in a year or so. Well, hold that pet "right" up there in front of you now. Visualize it! Feel it! I want you to be consumed by all of your new-found "rights" as you hear these next words.

Forget those rights!

You have absolutely no right to anything. You have no right to anything that demands that another person surrender either his time or his property to you for the fulfillment of your right.

You cannot receive health care unless some doctor or health practitioner surrenders some of his time — his life — to you. He may be willing to do this for compensation, but that's his choice. You have no "right" to his time or property. You have no right to his life.

You think you have some "right" to a job; a job with a living wage, whatever that is. Do you mean to tell me that you have a right to force your services on another person, and then the right to demand that this person compensate you with money? Sorry, forget it. I am sure you would scream if some urban outdoorsmen (that would be "homeless person" for those of you who don't want to give these less fortunate people a romantic and adventurous title) presented his smelly self to you and demanded *his* job and *your* money.

The people who have been telling you about all the rights you have are simply exercising one of theirs — the right to be an imbecile. Their being imbeciles didn't cost anyone else either property or time. It's their right, and they exercise it brilliantly.

By the way, did you catch my use of the phrase "less fortunate" a bit ago? When I was talking about the urban outdoorsmen? That phrase is a favorite of the Left. Think about it, and you'll understand why.

To imply that one person is homeless, destitute, dirty, drunk, spaced out on drugs, unemployable, and generally miserable because he is "less fortunate" is to imply that a successful person — one with a job, a home and a future — is in that position because he or she was "fortunate."

The dictionary says that *fortunate* means "having

derived good from an unexpected place." There is nothing unexpected about deriving good from hard work. There is also nothing unexpected about deriving misery from choosing drugs, alcohol, and the street.

If the Left can create the common perception that success and failure are simple matters of "fortune" or "luck," then it is easy to promote and justify their various income redistribution schemes. After all, we are just evening out the odds a little bit.

This "success equals luck" idea the Liberals like to push is seen everywhere. Remember Democratic Rep. Dick Gephardt's reference to high-income earners as "people who have won life's lottery?" You got it! They are making the big bucks because they were — all together now — *lucky*!

It's not luck, my friends. It's choice.

One of the greatest lessons I ever learned was in a book by Og Mandino, entitled *The Greatest Secret in the World*. The lesson? Very simple, really: "Use wisely your power of choice."

That bum sitting on a heating grate, smelling like a wharf, is there by choice. He is there because of the sum total of the choices he has made in his life. This truism is absolutely the hardest thing for some people to accept, especially those who consider themselves to be victims of something or other — victims of discrimination, bad luck, the system, capitalism, whatever. After all, nobody really wants to accept the blame for their position in life. Not when it is so much easier to point and say, "Look! *He* did this to me!" than it is to look into a mirror and say, "You S.O.B.! *You* did this to me!"

The key to accepting responsibility for your life is to accept the fact that your choices, every one of them, are leading you inexorably to either success or failure, however you define those terms.

Some of the choices are obvious: Whether or not to stay in school. Whether or not to get pregnant. Whether or not to hit the bottle. Whether or not to keep this job you hate until you get another better-paying job. Whether or not to save some of your money, or get that new car.

Some of the choices are seemingly insignificant: Whom to go to the movies with. Whose car to ride home in. Whether to watch the tube tonight, or read a book on investing.

But, and you can be sure of this, each choice counts. Each choice is a building block — some large, some small. But each one is a part of the structure.

If you make the right choices, or if you make more right

choices than wrong ones, something absolutely terrible may happen to you. Something unthinkable.   You, my friend, could become one of the hated, the evil, the ugly, the feared, the filthy, the successful, the rich. Quite a few people have made that mistake.

The rich basically serve two purposes in this country.

First, they provide the investments, the investment capital, and the brains for the formation of new businesses. Businesses that hire people. Businesses that send millions of paychecks home each week to the un-rich.

Second, the rich are a wonderful object of ridicule, distrust, and hatred. Nothing is more valuable to a politician than the envy most Americans feel for people with more than they.

Envy is a powerful emotion. Even more powerful than the emotional minefield that surrounds Bill Clinton when he judges a college cheerleading contest.

Politicians use envy to get votes and power. And they keep that power by promising the envious that the envied will be punished: "The rich will pay their fair share of taxes, if I have anything to do with it."

The truth is that the top 10% of income earners in this country pays almost 50% of all income taxes collected. I shudder to think what these job producers would be paying if our tax system were any more "fair."

You have heard, no doubt, that in America the rich get richer and the poor get poorer. Bull! That statement is provably false. The government's own numbers show that the poor actually get richer, and the rich, in large numbers, get poorer.

Let's assume, though, that this "rich get richer" bit is true. For some of the rich, it is true. Why? Because they keep doing the things that made them rich in the first place. Ditto for the poor. The rich keep saving their dollar bills, while the poor keep spending theirs.

Speaking of the poor, you should know that under our government's definition of "poor" you can have a $5 million net worth, a $300,000 home and a new $90,000 Mercedes, completely paid for, a maid, cook, and valet, and $1 million in your checking account, and you can still be officially defined by our government as "living in poverty." Now there's something you haven't seen on the evening news.

How does the government pull this one off? Very simple, really. To determine whether or not some poor soul is "living in poverty," the government measures one thing.

Just one thing. Income. It doesn't matter one bit how much you have, how much you own, how many cars you drive or how big they are, whether or not your pool is heated, whether you winter in Aspen and spend the summers in the Bahamas, or how much is in your savings account. It only matters how much income you claim in that particular year. This means that if you take a one-year leave of absence from your high-paying job and decide to live off the money in your savings and checking accounts while you write the next great American novel, the government says you are "living in poverty."

This isn't exactly what you had in mind when you heard these gloomy statistics, is it?

Do you need more convincing? Try this. The government's own statistics show that people who are said to be "living in poverty" spend more than $1.50 for each dollar of income they claim. Something is a bit fishy here. Just remember all this the next time Dan Rather puffs up and tells you about some hideous new poverty statistics.

Why has the government concocted this phony poverty scam? Because the government needs an excuse to grow, to expand its social welfare programs, which translates into an expansion of its power. If the government can convince you that the number of "poor" is increasing, it will have all the excuse it needs to sway an electorate suffering from the advanced stages of Obsessive-Compulsive Compassion Disorder.

I'm about to be stoned by the faculty here. They've already changed their minds about that honorary degree I was going to get. Sure, Kermit got one, but I'm not holding my breath.

That's OK, though. I still have my Ph.D. in Insensitivity from the Neal Boortz Institute for Insensitivity Training. I learned that, in short, sensitivity sucks. It's a trap. Think about it _ the truth knows no sensitivity. Life can be insensitive. Wallow too much in sensitivity and you can't deal with life, or the truth.

Get over it.

Now, before the dean has me shackled and hauled off, I have a few random thoughts.

• You need to register to vote, unless you are on welfare. If you are living off the efforts of others, please do us the favor of sitting down and shutting up until you are on your own again.

• When you do vote, your votes for the House and the

Senate are more important than your vote for president. The House controls the purse strings, so concentrate your awareness there.

- Liars cannot be trusted, even when the liar is the president of the United States. If someone can't deal honestly with you, send them packing.

- Don't bow to the temptation to use the government as an instrument of plunder. If it is wrong for you to take money from someone else who earned it, to take their money by force for your own needs, then it is certainly just as wrong for you to demand that the government step forward and do this dirty work for you.

- Don't look in other people's pockets. You have no business there. What they earn is theirs. What your earn is yours. Keep it that way. Nobody owes you anything, except to respect your privacy and leave you the hell alone.

- Speaking of earning, the revered 40-hour work week is for losers. Forty hours should be considered the minimum, not the maximum. You don't see highly successful people clocking out of the office every afternoon at five. The losers are the ones caught up in that afternoon rush hour. The winners drive home in the dark.

- Free speech is meant to protect unpopular speech. Popular speech, by definition, needs no protection.
- Finally (and aren't you glad to hear that word), as Og Mandino wrote,
  1. Proclaim your rarity. Each of you is a rare and unique human being.
  2. Use wisely your power of choice.
  3. Go the extra mile . . . drive home in the dark.

Oh, and put off buying a television set as long as you can.

Now, if you have any idea at all what's good for you, you will get the hell out of here and never come back. Class dismissed.

DEBUGGING THE
New Graduate

Now that you have finished "listening" to my commencement speech that has precious little chance of ever actually being delivered to a graduating class, it's time for you to grab that diploma, hang that tassel from your rear-view mirror, and head out into the real world. If you harbor any idea at all that the academic environment you have been steeping in for the past four years or so bears any working resemblance to the real world, you have one big surprise waiting for you.

Did you think college was tough? Well, five years from now, if you have any ambition at all, you are going to look back on your college years as an extended party. Now the real work starts.

The remaining chapters of this book were originally referred to as "Reprogramming Tips," but something about that title just didn't work for me. It's not that these chapters are an attempt to reprogram so much as they are an attempt to debug. Your mind has already been programmed by your professors and your classmates with ideas, beliefs and concepts that cannot stand up to fact or reality. The intent of these chapters is to debug some of this programming.

You are going to have facts, figures, percentages, and other ideas thrown at you in the following chapters. There will be no extensive footnotes or references as to where these facts and figures came from.

In the 28 years that I have been doing talk radio shows, I estimate that I have read more than 30,000 newspapers, 5,000 news magazines, 40,000 special reports and articles from various think tanks, 450 books, and almost 250,000 letters and telefaxes.

In reading all of these newspapers and what-not, certain facts and figures have been burned and re-burned into my mind. Some of them are regurgitated for you here.

A good example would be the percentage of privately owned handguns in the United States that are actually used in a murder. I remember those figures from year to year, but that doesn't mean I can tell you what study they came from or where I first learned the statistics.[1]

So, I'll just tell you the same thing that I tell the listeners to my radio show several times a week: Don't believe anything that I offer here. That's not to say that I am deliberately trying to mislead you. I could never have maintained the confidence and trust of a radio audience over nearly three decades if I had a habit of fudging on the facts or trying to mislead listeners.

If you read something here that sparks your curiosity or imagination, go out and gather some additional information on your own. If you put some effort into trying to prove or to disprove the ideas set forth here, then that information will be all the more valuable to you.

For 28 years I have been inviting my listeners to nail me if they find me distorting the facts or trying to mislead them. For 28 years I have remained un-nailed.

The same invitation is now extended to you.

Now, let's get on with the debugging.

---

[1]Just for drill . . . I am providing a blank here. Write down in that blank the percentage of privately owned handguns, legal and illegal, in the United States that you believe were used in a murder in 1995. Here's your blank_____%. OK, great! We'll see how you did a bit later.

WHAT'S ALL THIS
About A Democracy?

We start out with a real challenge. In this chapter I'm going to get rid of one of the most insidious ideas that has made its way into the minds of, I dare say, the vast majority of Americans — the idea that this country was designed as and is supposed to be a democracy.

Don't worry. I can handle this one without a net.

Throughout your lifetime you have continually heard the United States referred to as a "democracy." And during this time you have heard the idea of democracy presented in nothing but the most favorable and glowing terms.

I am sure that you are absolutely convinced that the United States is a democracy. I am just as certain that you believe this is exactly what was intended by the people who founded this country.

Stand by for a surprise: You're wrong.

The word *democracy* does not appear anywhere in the Declaration of Independence. The word democracy does not appear anywhere in our Constitution, nor does it appear in any of the constitutions of the fifty states.

More surprises: Our Founding Fathers — people with names like Thomas Jefferson, John Jay, Benjamin Franklin, and Alexander Hamilton — did not think of the idea of a democracy in very positive terms at all. In fact, they had some quite nasty things to say about the concept.

You will also be surprised to know that it was the official policy of the government of the United States, right up until the 1930s, to teach the soldiers of the U.S. armed forces that a democracy was a dangerous and undesirable form of government that would lead to mob rule and the end of private property rights.[1]

Something changed, though.

Suddenly, in the past 60 years, we have come to believe that the United States was formed as a democracy, that it is supposed to be a democracy, and that democracy is the

---

[1] A hint. Find an old copy — one published in the 1930s — of the U.S. Army Field Training Manual and read the political definitions soldiers were required to learn. Somehow this all got changed around the time of FDR which, coincidently, was about the time that our presidents started using the "D" word.

---

way to go when it comes to governments. Every one of your college professors probably believed this. They should know better, but that's another story.

OK. You're probably just a bit confused here. This "democracy" idea has been pounded into your head for quite some time now, and it's hard to consider, let along accept, the idea that there actually may be something wrong with the concept.

About 200 years ago a professor named Alexander Tyler had a thing or two to say about democracies. This was at a time when the 13 original colonies were still under British control. Since the United States didn't then exist, Tyler was hardly writing about our own government. Instead, he was writing about the fall of the Athenian Republic nearly 2,000 years earlier. Little did Professor Tyler realize how his words would apply to the United States more than 200 years later. Professor Tyler's observations are quite sobering:

"A Democracy cannot exist as a permanent form of government. It can exist only until the voters discover that they can vote themselves largesse[2] from the public treasury. From that moment on, the majority always votes for the candidates

---

[2]Look it up. It will do you good.

promising the most benefits from the public treasury, with the result that a Democracy always collapses over loose fiscal policy, always followed by a Dictatorship.

"*The average age of the world's greatest civilizations has been 200 years. These nations have progressed through this sequence: From bondage to spiritual faith; from spiritual faith to great courage; from courage to liberty; from liberty to abundance; from abundance to selfishness; from selfishness to complacency; from complacency to apathy; from apathy to dependency; from dependency back into bondage.*"

Now, I think we're somewhere around the complacency/apathy part of this progression right now. We damn sure aren't anywhere close to that "courage" part.

So, if we're not a democracy, just what are we?

Good question, and there's a good answer: We are a "constitutional republic."

What's the difference?

Don't go running to a current dictionary to check the definitions of these words. The definition you would find for *democracy* will be quite a bit different from the definition of 30 or 40 years ago.

A democracy is, simply put, a system where the majority rules. Whatever the majority wants, the majority gets.

"OK," you say, "so the majority rules in a democracy. How is that different from what we do? We have elections, and the person with the most votes wins. Isn't that a democracy?"

Not exactly. In the United States there are some very specific rules (the Constitution) that must be followed by everybody. It doesn't matter whether you're a sheep-dipper in Utah or a senator in Washington, these constitutional rules apply to you.

The basic rules, of course, deal with our rights to our lives, our liberty, and our property.

Under our Constitution you cannot be deprived of your life, liberty, or property just because the majority of people think it might be a good idea. The whim of the majority is subject to the law. If we were a true democracy, the majority could get together and decide that your home should be taken away and you should be killed. "But wait!" you protest. "I haven't done anything! I have a right to a trial!" Sorry, pal. This is a democracy. The majority rules.

There is an excellent example in our recent history to illustrate the basic difference between a democracy and a constitutional republic.

In the South, prior to the civil rights movement and the

1964 Civil Rights Act, democracy was the rule. The majority of people were white, and the white majority had little or no respect for any which the black minority had relative to property, or even to their own lives. The majority — the mob — ruled.

Then along came some people who believed that the rights of black Americans to control their lives, their property, and their basic freedom should be protected, and were, in fact, protected by our Constitution, against the wishes of the Southern majority.

The people of the United States came to the realization that, in the South, the white majority did not rule. The *law*, not the people, was supreme. Blacks had rights under our Constitution, regardless of the will of the majority.

Democracy was out, and the rule of law was back in.

To put it in even more basic terms, a lynch mob is a democracy. There are 51 people there. Fifty of those people think that the remaining person should swing from an oak tree. Person No. 51 doesn't think a whole hell of a lot of the idea, but he's in the minority. The majority wins. The mob rules. No. 51 swings.

Simpler still: A democracy is three wolves and one sheep voting on what's for dinner.

Don't get me wrong. I'm not bashing democratic processes. In our country we make certain decisions such as the election of our representatives, bond issues, and other matters based on a vote. The side that gets the most votes wins. But these democratic processes cannot, and should not, be used to deprive people of their basic rights.

So, why all this democracy-bashing? Why is all of this so important?

If you check our history, you will find that our politicians became fond of referring to the United States as a democracy just about the time they became similarly fond of the idea of big government and redistributing wealth.

Our elected officials recognized that they could become more and more powerful if they had more government goodies to hand out. They knew that the government cannot give away anything unless it first takes that thing from whoever earned it or owns it. But to take that thing (money, for instance) from the person who earned or produced it would be a violation of that person's right to his property.

Well, let's call ourselves a democracy! That way, when we take someone's property to give to someone else, we can say that what we are doing is really OK because it's what the people want. It's for the common good.

It's not really too tough to get more than 50% of the people to approve a scheme whereby the government will take property away from the wealthiest 30% of the people in this country and distribute it to the remaining 70%. Sounds like a great idea to those on the receiving end. It's not all that great a concept to the 30% who are getting ripped off, but, hell, we're a democracy! The majority rules! That's what we do!

Let's not belabor the point. My goal is to have this idea of mob rule flash through your mind every time you hear a politician speak of our "democracy." Maybe you'll also wonder, for a second or two, if that politician truly knows what he's talking about.

Those of you who become convinced, through your own thought processes and research, of the dangers of a democracy might be compelled to challenge the next person you hear use that word. Especially if that person is a teacher, a politician, or someone in a comparable position of authority. Just ask him, "Excuse me, but what makes you think our country is a democracy, or that it was even supposed to be a democracy? I've looked, and I can't find the word anywhere in our Declaration of Independence or Constitution."

You, like me, will get to the point that you just love to watch those people squirm.

Remember, lynch mobs are democracies. Maybe you'll think we deserve something better.

BUSINESSES
Don't Pay Taxes

Those of you who have been living in the shelter of the education environment are about to get a form of sticker shock. We'll just call it paycheck stub shock. Just *wait* until you see what the government does to your check.

Have you heard people, especially politicians, talk about businesses needing to carry more of the tax burden? You probably think that's a good idea, don't you? Those huge corporations should pay more taxes so that the little people can keep more of their own money to spend.

Some serious debugging needs to be done here.

Consider these points:

1. There is absolutely no limit at all to the government's desire for your money. The politicians want as much

of your money as they can possibly get their hands on, and they will keep reaching into your pocket and grabbing your cash right up to the point where they start to seriously fear you are about to cut their hands off.

2. The politicians will use any subterfuge, any lie, any trick they can, to keep you from realizing just how much government is really costing you.

When politicians think they have pushed the individual taxpayers to the breaking point, they will start to talk about raising taxes on businesses and those evil corporations.

Washington believes that the average American actually thinks that businesses and corporations pay taxes. Unfortunately, Washington is right; the average American thinks just that.

But the average American is dead wrong.

Learn this well: **The only entity in this country that pays taxes is the *individual*! Corporations and businesses do not pay taxes. They *collect* taxes from individuals and pass them on to the government.**

Virtually every economist in this country who is not

working for the government[1] will concur with this statement.

On second thought, maybe I had better expand on that. Let's try again: Virtually every economist in this country who is not working for the government or teaching in a college or university will concur with this statement.

When a business or corporation takes money out of corporate earnings to send off to the government in the form of taxes, that money has to be diverted from some other account.

If the money had not been paid to the government as taxes, it clearly would have been used for some other purpose. The money could have been used to pay salaries, give employees raises, pay stockholder dividends, pay profits to owners, buy raw materials, have a company barbecue, put new leather upholstery in the corporate jet . . . you get the general idea. Sending that money to Washington means it isn't going to be spent by that company somewhere else.

Now, if the money paid to the government was going to be used for salaries, just where did that money actually

---

[1] An important distinction. Government economists are being paid to preach the government mantra. They shoot shoot straight with you on this and they are suddenly looking for jobs in the private sector.

come from? Those dollars came right out of the pockets of the employees who would have received a raise or who would have been hired.

OK, so what if no raises or new hiring were in the picture? Then the money might have been paid to stockholders as dividends, or to the owners as profit. Either way, the money is still coming from an individual — the individual stockholder or the owner.

Whenever a dollar is spent, it eventually filters down to an individual somewhere. The person who provides the beef or the plastic forks for the employee barbecue. The workers who built the stomach pump used on half the staff the night of the company barbecue. The man who stitches the new leather upholstery in the business jet. Or the farmer who raised the cow that gave up its life for the cause of hamburgers and comfortable corporate posteriors.

Our economy operates for the benefit of individuals. All profits and earnings are eventually spent to benefit individuals, and all costs of doing business are eventually paid by individuals.

The individual is the basic unit of our economy.

So, when a corporation pays a dollar in taxes, that dollar eventually comes from some individual's pocket.

When taxes are raised on corporations or businesses, those taxes are paid by individuals somewhere. The employee who goes without the raise. The person who doesn't get hired. The stockholder who sees his dividend decrease. The farmer who can't get a good price for his cow.

Somewhere an individual human being pays. The business or corporation collects the money, and off it goes to Washington.

So, when you hear some politician yammering about the need to raise taxes on businessmen and rich corporations, that politician is talking about raising *your* taxes.

Just for the hell of it, you should drop him a line and let him know that you're on to him.

WHO REALLY Pays The Taxes?

When Bill Clinton was running for president the first time, he talked about his plan to raise taxes on the "rich" so that they would be paying "their fair share." This proved to be extremely popular with both the voters and most of the talking heads in the media.

Clinton and his supporters also loved to refer to the 1980s as the "decade of greed." This painted a picture of evil, greedy rich people lining their pockets during the '80s while the rest of the poor oppressed Americans picked up the load on income taxes and saw their fortunes dwindle. This all added up to a spectacular election victory.

This same picture of greed and the evil lifestyle of the rich has probably been painted by many of the professors in your college or university. Clinton knew better. It may be that your professors did not.

Well, here's the antidote for this anti-achievement venom you've been fed. If, after you read this, you still believe those professors were right, you ought to go back to the old alma mater and teach with them.

Bashing the rich works. It gets votes. It works because of two factors: ignorance and envy. This "pay their fair share" and "decade of greed" nonsense certainly sounds great to people who don't have the slightest clue of who is paying what in income taxes. It also appeals to those who cannot contain their jealousy and envy for those who have more than they do.

Before you read any further, try this little test. Believe me, the remainder of this chapter will mean so much more to you if you will just play along for a second.

There are two blanks for you to fill in below. In the first blank I want you to pencil in the percentage of total income taxes collected by the federal government that you think are paid by those people in the top 1% of all income earners. In the second blank I want you to pencil in the percentage of total income taxes you think are paid by the top 10% of all income earners.

Give it a shot.

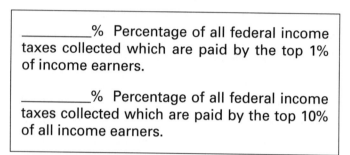

_____% Percentage of all federal income taxes collected which are paid by the top 1% of income earners.

_____% Percentage of all federal income taxes collected which are paid by the top 10% of all income earners.

My guess is that you were off. Way off. You are probably in another galaxy. In fact, I would go so far as to say that if you were anywhere close to the actual figure, it is only because you are one of those mindless people who listens to those hate-filled radio talk show hosts.

The actual figures?

The top 1% of all income earners in the United States earns about 13.8% of all of the income. They pay about 28.7% of all of the income taxes collected.

Are you believing this? The top 1% pays almost 30% of all income taxes paid in this country! And they only earn 14% of the income!

Moving on. . .. The top 10% of the income earners earns about 39% of all income, but they pay about 58.8% of all income taxes collected.

Just a little amazed, aren't you? Just 10% of the income earners in this country paying almost 60% of the taxes! Wow!

But, wait a minute. Maybe they sweetened their deal during those horrible Reagan years. That's it! They used to pay more, and now they're paying less.

Sorry. Doesn't wash. At the beginning of 1983, when all of the nice Reagan tax cuts were taking place, the top 1% was paying just 20.3% of the taxes and the top 10% was paying 49.7%. The share of the income taxes the rich paid during the "decade of greed"[1] actually went up!

Now, that should take care of the "not paying their fair share" idea. The higher income earners are obviously paying a much higher share of the income taxes than those in the middle or lower income groups.

What about this "decade of greed" idea that Clinton, his

---

[1] We are measuring the "decade of greed" as the ten years immediately preceding the ascendancy of William Jefferson "Slick Willie" Clinton to the Oval Office.

myrmidons[2] in the media, and your professors have been pushing for the Reagan years? Was there a real need for some knight in shining armor to come sleazing out of Arkansas and punish these evil rich people for the hideous tax breaks they got during the '80s?

To see if these rich people were making things easier on themselves during the Reagan years, you would want to know whether they ended up paying a greater or lesser share of the total taxes collected at the end of that period.

Guess what? In spite of what your professors have probably been telling you for the past four years, and in spite of what Clinton and his followers have been preaching, from 1983 to 1993 the percentage share of the total income taxes collected by the U.S. government went *up* for all taxpayers in the top 1%, the top 10%, the top 25%, and the top 50%. It went *down* (from 7.2% to 4.8%) only for the bottom 50% of all income earners.

By any measure this does not reflect greed,[3] nor does it

---

[2] Look it up. *Myrmidon* is an absolutely fantastic word. Just because you are out of college doesn't mean you can toss your dictionary.

[3] The word "greed " is incapable of definition. Logic will destroy any definition you can find. The word is actually a weapon used by the Left to create instantaneous feelings of outrage and hatred toward the person who is saddled with the derogatory description.

---

support the idea that the rich are not paying their fair share.

So, were these figures available to Clinton when he was talking up his tax increase? You bet they were. He knew the facts. The media knew the facts. But the facts didn't matter. Clinton was playing the numbers, the election numbers, and the game was working too well for anyone (in the media, for instance) to come along and douse the fire.

I don't want this to be a civics class, but a brief lesson in the numbers of elections will help you to understand why politicians are always so quick to propose tax increases for the rich and tax cuts for the middle class.

When you propose a big tax increase on the nasty, filthy rich, you know that you are making points with about 90% of the voters. Sure, the high income earners aren't exactly toasting you at dinner, but they have only about 10% of the votes, and they probably were not going to vote for you anyway. So, what have you got to lose? Nail 'em, and watch the votes pour in.

If you propose a tax decrease on the middle class. . . no problem! The middle class loves it, and they will have more money to spend that will benefit the businesses that are, more likely than not, owned or serviced by those nasty rich people.

Politicians want to stay in power. To do that they need votes. The surest way to get the largest number of votes is to buy them. To get the money you need to buy these votes you take it away from the people whose votes you *do not* need. . . and you give that money to, or spend that money on goodies for, the people with the votes you do need.

It's all so completely simple.

No wonder the rich are paying such a huge proportion of the taxes. They have the money that the politicians need but not the votes. The lower income people have the votes but not the money. Guess who gets nailed.

Now you will never again be able to listen to politicians whine about the rich not paying their fair share of taxes without rolling your eyes.

Yet another step into the real world.

GROUND
Rush

et's talk for a minute about Social Security.

Hold on now. I know that as soon as you read the words *Social Security* your immediate thought was to put down this book and pick up something more interesting. Almost any of the junk mail you received today will do. You think this topic is excruciatingly boring. Only blue-hairs and wizened, toothless old men are worried about Social Security.

Well, you don't have blue hair and you aren't sure what *wizened* means, so this isn't for you. You sit there smugly thinking that you are far too young to be worried about Social Security.

So let me tell you about "ground rush."

It's a skydiving term. When you go through training to jump out of perfectly serviceable airplanes, you learn about ground rush … and you learn how it can kill you flat dead.

Just a few seconds after jumping out of an airplane, you will be falling at about 120 miles per hour. Here's the strange part: you don't really believe you are falling! You think that you must be caught in some type of updraft. You just aren't getting any closer to the ground. Or so you think.

Skydivers learn to recognize this little mind trick and to guard against it. They know that as they near the ground it will suddenly – very suddenly – appear as if the ground is rushing up to meet them at a terrific speed. If they haven't pulled the rip cord and deployed their parachute, it may be just a tad late. The consequences aren't very pretty and can take a long time to clean up.

You may have experienced a variation of ground rush on expressways. That bridge way down the road doesn't look like it's getting any closer. Suddenly it rushes toward you and disappears behind you. Bridge rush.

When you were in school you probably experienced "finals rush." That final exam seemed so far away, so you delayed studying (pulling the rip cord). Suddenly that exam came screaming across the calendar and you found you didn't have time to do the studying you honestly intended to do.

So why is ground rush important to you?

Because somewhere out there, down the road a bit, is that time of your life called "retirement." Right now retirement seems so far away that you can't really conceive of ever getting there. You're not really falling. The ground isn't really getting any closer.

Just as the ground will seemingly accelerate toward the skydiver, or the bridge to the driver, or the final exam to the unwary college student, so will your eventual retirement suddenly appear down the road, rushing toward you with blinding speed.

Time accelerates. You won't believe how fast.

If you don't already have your parachute open, it's going to be quite an impact.

Over the next few years there will be much debate in Washington on what to do about Social Security. You will be affected, strongly affected, by what happens in that debate, so you had damned well better pay close attention.

The Social Security debate ... it's not just for geezers anymore.

So read, now, about Social Security and how the government is sabotaging your best chance for a comfortable retirement with deficit spending.

You're just out of school, but it's already a lot later than you think.

YOUR PAYCHECK: Your Employer "Contributes" Nothing!

Y ou had better start thinking about retirement sooner, rather than later, or your "golden" years are going to be spent scratching yourself while sitting on the crude wooden deck you built outside your double-wide and watching your neighbor tinker with his rusted-out Camaro.

You need to understand this right now: Social Security *isn't* going to cut it. You would be better off depending on a lottery ticket to provide you with a comfortable retirement.

The system is broke, folks. The way the law stands now, you are going to pay far more into Social Security than you could ever hope to take out. Unless, that is, you manage to qualify for Social Security Disability payments right off the bat by, say, getting maimed as an innocent bystander in an ethics complaint–filing contest between David Bonior and Newt Gingrich.

If a private company were running this Social Security scam on the American people, its officers and employees would all be arrested and charged with heinous crimes against humanity.

If, however, the Political Class would let you take all of that money you are going to flush into the Social Security System and instead invest it in stocks and bonds (real big "if" here), you would end up with five to ten times more retirement income. That could be the difference between your double-wide in Podunk and a condo on the beach at Ft. Lauderdale.

As soon as you start your first job (if you haven't already), the government starts working one of its slickest scams on you: You are told that your employer is going to "match" your Social Security "contribution."

Two things: First, it isn't a "contribution"; it's a tax. Contributions are voluntary; Social Security taxes are not. Second, your employer isn't matching *anything*. Every single penny paid to Social Security on your account is coming straight out of your pocket.

When an employer makes a decision to hire you, he

budgets a certain amount for your employment. That amount is based on several considerations including the prevailing market for your particular job skills, how much money he has available, and your economic value to his business.

To illustrate: Let's say your employer determines that he can budget $40,000 for the cost of your employment. Does that mean that you are going to be paid $40,000 a year? Hardly.

Think about it this way. If you determine that you have $600 a month to set aside for the expenses associated with automobile ownership, are you going to go out and buy a car that has monthly payments of $600? Not if you've learned anything these past few years.

If you blow your entire automobile budget on payments, where are the insurance payments going to come from? What about gas? Maintenance? Tires? That pesky yearly license tag? You had better leave room in the budget for those goodies.

Well, your employer has to leave room in his budget for the various costs associated with putting you on his payroll. This is all going to come out of the $40,000 a year he has budgeted for the cost of your employment.

Just a partial list of the costs of your employment includes unemployment insurance, worker's compensation insurance, health benefits, paid vacations, parking, even the cost of the coffee you get from the employee's coffee cave every morning. Believe me, it adds up.

Oh. . . and one more thing. His "matching contribution" to your Social Security tax comes out of the budget, too.

When all is said and cried over, he may have about $34,000 left from the $40,000 he budgeted to put you on the payroll. Guess what — *that's* your salary.

Your gross salary will equal whatever remains of the amount your boss budgeted for your employment *after* he has paid all of the costs incurred by putting you on the payroll.

This nonsense of splitting up your Social Security tax into your "share" and your employer's "share" is a blatant scam set up by the Political Class to keep you from realizing the true cost of this absurd income redistribution program.

It's your money. All of it. And you'll be damned lucky to ever see it again.

Every time that money disappears from your paycheck, spend a few moments thinking of how you could be investing those dollars for your own retirement.

IT'S *THEIR* SOCIAL SECURITY
But it's *Your* Retirement

So far the debugging ideas in the book may have amused you. Maybe they made you a little curious. Maybe they actually sparked an idea here and there. Well, stand by because this chapter should make you drop-dead furious.

After reading the last chapter you now understand that the total amount paid to the Social Security scheme under your name — both the amount taken directly out of your paycheck and the amount the government is trying to con you into believing was "contributed" by your employer — comes directly out of your pocket. You paid it. All of it.

To put it another way, there are no virgins paying Social Security taxes.

If you are just getting out of college, you have approximately 45 years to work. That means you will be retiring in about the year 2042. You should know that the year 2042 is about 13 years after the Social Security system is scheduled to go broke. You read right — 13 years!

Did you catch that word? *Broke.* No money. The system into which you will have paid thousands of dollars a year will be broke!

If we can count on history as a guide to the future, our wonderful government will try to solve this problem by (1) increasing the retirement age to 75 or so, in hopes that the system will be saved because so many people will take the dirt nap before they can qualify for benefits; or, (2) by raising Social Security taxes another couple of percentage points to put off the inevitable bankruptcy. I'm sure either of the plans would be just fine with you.

Oh, I almost forgot. They are also considering a system whereby you don't get *any* Social Security benefits at all if you lived your life responsibly enough that you can provide for yourself after retirement. You still pay the taxes. You just don't get the benefits.

Isn't your government wonderful? Believe me, it gets worse.

About 15 years ago our federal government made a bit of a mistake. It allowed some local governments around the country to pull their employees out of the Social Security system. Many governments took the hint and ran like hell.

Some local governments that opted out of the Social Security scheme allowed their employees to do their own retirement planning. Others instituted pension, retirement, and other plans that did not mirror Social Security at all.

But three Texas counties did something unique when they pulled their employees out of Social Security. They continued to require those employees to pay exactly the same amount into a retirement/disability plan as they were previously paying to Social Security. The counties also "matched" those payments, just as your employer would. This means, just as with Social Security, that the entire amount was effectively being paid by the employee.

OK, so how did the employees in these three counties do?

Let's use Galveston County, Texas, as the example.[1] (The other two Texas counties that followed suit were Brazoria and Matagorda.)

---

[1] These figures are so spectacular I wouldn't blame you if you thought I was feeding you a big one. *This* time I'll tell you where I got them. They came from Brief Analysis No. 215 of the National Center for Policy Analysis in Washington, D.C. I'm not sure, but I think these people analyze politics.

Galveston County employees voted to get out of the Social Security system in 1981. Each employee's new contribution to the retirement system was 13.78%, very close to the old Social Security contribution. Of that amount, 9.737% was paid into each employee's private individual retirement account, which returned a 6.5% interest, compounded daily. The remainder was used to pay disability and life insurance premiums to cover employees in case of an accident or premature arrival at room temperature.

I know, numbers can be dry and boring. Well, the results of Galveston County's retirement plan are anything *but* dry and boring. Wait till you see what happens to Galveston County employees when they reach retirement age.

First example — a county employee on the low end of the scale, making about $20,000 a year. If this person were to rely on Social Security, he would be getting the princely sum of $775 per month. Wow! What a deal!

This county employee is lucky, though, because he has the Galveston County Alternate Plan. Instead of $775 per month, he gets $2,740 a month.

What about higher-paid county employees — the professional types, engineers, administrators, etc.? A Galveston

County employee who was making about $50,000 a year would get about $1,302 per month from Social Security. That's about $15,600 a year. But (oh happy day!) he doesn't have to rely on Social Security. The Alternate Plan is going to pay him $6,843 a month. That's $82,000 a year compared to $15,600!

There's more.

Under Social Security, when a worker dies there is a one-time death benefit paid to his survivors — the horse-choking sum of $255. Under the Galveston plan that worker's survivors get a life insurance payment equal to three times his salary. The minimum is $50,000 with a $150,000 maximum.

Just one more brutal fact to make sure you realize what a jam this ridiculous system is in. In 1950, when your parents might have been starting grade school, there were 16 people working and paying their Social Security taxes for every person receiving benefits.

Today, in 1997, there are about 3.3 people working and paying for every person on the taking end. By the year 2030, the ratio will be less than two to one.

Think of it this way: It's one thing when 100 people go together to buy a yacht, but if 98 of them die and leave the remaining two with the full cost of yacht ownership, you're going to see a "for sale" sign real quick.

The problem is obvious, so you are probably wondering why it isn't being fixed.

Let's see how clear I can make this.

The largest single identifiable block of voters in this country is Social Security recipients. These are the people who drive the impossibly large cars right down the center of the busiest street in town — at 20 miles per hour — on the third day of every month, on the way to deposit their Social Security checks. They are the sole remaining support for the white glove industry.

You had better believe, these people vote! But they vote on basically two issues — Social Security and Medicare. They couldn't care less about term limits, balanced budgets, human rights in China, family-leave laws, EPA cleanup sites, and nuclear non-proliferation. They care about Social Security and Medicare. Beyond that, they have no use for politicians.

So here you have the recipe for catastrophe: an extremely large block of voters with their votes clearly for sale to the senator or representative who will make them feel the most secure about their Social Security and Medicare payments.

Do you really think these senators and representatives are going to care that you are being ripped off by this system? First of all, they are fairly certain that you don't have a clue what is going on. Secondly, they know that your kind doesn't vote. At least you don't vote in numbers anywhere near big enough to offset the blue-hairs.

Bottom line: Your congressmen and senators are taking your money, by legal force, and using that money to buy votes from Seasoned Citizens who won't be around to *tsk-tsk* when you discover that there isn't actually a Social Security account in your name, and that you aren't going to collect a thing.

There are various Social Security privatization plans being discussed right now, and this is going to be a very hot issue over the next few years. Get involved. Read. Learn. It's your retirement they're discussing out there.

Oh, and by the way. . . When you hear about plans to allow the government to take Social Security funds and invest them in the stock market to pay future benefits that's tantamount to partial government ownership of private business. And that, by definition, is socialism.

Just thought I'd point that little goodie out to you.

ABOUT
Race

You can't escape it. America is consumed with the issue of race. And there definitely *is* a race problem in this country. You need look no further than the reactions we saw from different racial groups when the infamous O.J. Simpson "not guilty" verdict was announced.

Just imagine, for a moment, the tremendous things that could be accomplished by *all* of the people of this country if we could stop moaning and gnashing our teeth over racial and cultural differences and interact harmoniously with each other. Our problems need to be worked through and solved.

Hopefully you learned in school that the first step in solving any problem is (duh!) identifying the problem. If you spend a few hundred dollars working on your car's engine, only to find out that the problem was with the transmission, you should feel appropriately stupid.

Identify the problem!

The same rule applies to solving our race "problem."

Is it racism? Maybe it's prejudice! It could be bigotry! Maybe even culturalism! All four are different problems, and all four beg for different solutions. Nothing I have to say is going to solve our problem of race, but I will make you this one promise: After you have read this chapter, a little bell will go off somewhere between your ears every time you hear anyone use the word *racism*. You will also find that you use that word a bit less often yourself.

Fact: Fewer than one in 100 people who use the words racist or racism would be able to accurately define them.

Do you think you can define racism? Give it a try. Turn your eyes and do it now.

You're wrong. I'd bet on it.

Until recently, almost any dictionary you picked up would have a definition of *racism* that read something like this:

> **Racism.** n. 1. A belief in the inherent genetic superiority of one race of people over another and a belief in the right of the superior group to dominate that racial group believed to be inferior.

The key to any legitimate definition of *racism* is that the racist group or individual believes that it, or he, is genetically superior to the other group.

You can dislike someone, or some group, without feeling that you are inherently or genetically superior to them. You can distrust them, fear them, scorn them, run from them, avoid them, all without adopting a belief in your supposed genetic superiority. . . all without being racist.

So, why is this all so important?

Think about it. If you want solutions, first identify the problem!

Most of the differences that divide Blacks and Whites in America are based on culture, not genetics or skin color.

A white woman is sitting in her car at a stoplight. She sees a young black male approaching. She hits that little button that locks all of the car doors. The young black man hears the *thunk* and thinks to himself, "Racist."

Did that woman lock those doors because she believed in the inherent, genetic superiority of whites over blacks? Hardly. It's more likely that she locked her doors because she was aware that a disproportionate number of young black males commits violent crimes. She doesn't believe that this crime rate exists in young black males because of their skin color. Instead, she suspects it probably has something to do with the cultural influences on this man while he was growing up.

Another example: I own a hardware store and I'm looking for help. Two young men answer my want ad. One young man, who happens to be white, shows up neatly dressed. He carries himself well and has a good command of the English language. The other young man, black, shows up with baggy shorts worn 10 inches below his navel and high-top tennis shoes with laces flopping all over the place. His baseball hat is on backwards,[1] the price tag is still attached, and he has absolutely no communications skills.

Surprise, surprise, surprise: I hire the young white guy. The young black man is absolutely convinced that he didn't get the job because he was black. He didn't get the job because I am a racist.

Is that why I didn't hire the black man? Was it because I believed that the white applicant was genetically superior to

---

[1] It is a proven scientific fact that a person's IQ drops immediately by more than ten points as soon as that person puts on a baseball hat backwards. If you don't believe it, just sit somewhere and watch the behavior of people who are wearing their baseball hats this way.

the black applicant? Or was it because I made a judgment, based on attitude and appearance, that the young white man would make a better employee than the black man?

It really isn't difficult to understand why some people are so eager to blame each and every speed-bump that gets in their way on racism.

If you're a minority and you don't get a job you want, it is not only easier, but also more comfortable to blame it on racism. You can't do anything about your skin color. If you aren't getting these jobs because of your skin color, then there's really nothing you can do about it.

But if you didn't have a different skin pigmentation to fall back on as an excuse, you might have to consider other reasons why you didn't get the job. Maybe you didn't have the necessary skills. Maybe you have a slovenly appearance. Maybe you can't communicate effectively. Maybe you don't have the right job experience.

Gee... maybe it's you and not your color!

Do you know what that means? It means that you have to clean up! You might have to find some clothes that fit correctly. You might have to get some job experience before you apply for the better jobs. You might have to return to school to learn some of those things that were being taught back when you thought learning wasn't "cool" enough for you.

All of these things take time. They take work. They make you responsible for *your* destiny!

What a burden. At this point you're not at all sure you want to be responsible for your own destiny. What if you fail? What if you don't make it?

Failure would be so embarrassing, and you would have to take the responsibility. Man, it sure was easier just to blame it on racism.

Certainly there are true racists out there, but I have never met a person who believed in the genetic superiority of one race over another that I thought had an IQ approaching that of a slug.

Just *look* at these people! The greatest cultural event most bona fide racists have been to is a truck pull. They are hideous cretins and, thankfully, few and far between.

Let's just try to be more careful about throwing around the "R" word. When you let a person use racism as an excuse for every personal tragedy, failure, and problem that comes along, then you are aiding and abetting that person in his quest to hide from reality and to avoid the responsibility that he has for his own life and his own success.

If you want to see friends succeed, and you know that they must alter their behavior somewhat to succeed, then you are doing them no favors if you accept their excuses for their poor behavior.

Let's get on with solving the problems we face. . . together.

LIBERAL OR Conservative?

Twenty-eight years of engaging in verbal combat with tens of thousands of people on various issues has enabled me to answer, once and for all, one of the questions that may be confounding you: What is the difference between a Liberal and a Conservative?

For clarification, when I talk about "Conservatives" I am *not* talking about the so-called religious right or the Christian Coalition crowd. Those folks have their own agenda, and it isn't particularly friendly to my basic concept of freedom. They are referred to as conservatives primarily by people who wish to discredit true Conservatives through the association.

Having said that, the fundamental differences between the Left and the Right aren't really all that hard to understand. In a nutshell — here they are:

Liberals operate from a foundation of emotion and feelings.

Conservatives operate from a foundation of logic and facts.

Liberals view people in terms of their membership in groups.

Conservatives view people as individuals.

When Liberals talk about governmental or social issues, they talk in terms of how they "feel." When Conservatives discuss the same issues, they speak in terms of what they "think." Liberals talk of the need for compassion and empathy. They boast of their caring attitude and the kindness they spread wherever they go.

Liberals seldom use logical thought processes or accurate facts to back up their policies; not while they can just rely on the idea of "feeling the pain" of the people they obsess over. I call this weeping and moaning attitude "Obsessive-Compulsive Compassion Disorder."

As pointed out earlier in this book, it is terribly easy to show the entire world what a wonderfully compassionate and caring person you are when you can demonstrate your compassion and caring attitude by spending someone else's money instead of your own.

While Liberals are wallowing in their compassion and feelings, Conservatives rely on the cold, harsh reality of facts and logic to discuss the role of government and various government programs. When Conservatives step forward with the statistics and facts needed to back up their points and ideas, Liberals throw temper tantrums. They start screaming about "hate" and "extremism" and try to paint their conservative tormentors as evil and mean spirited.

This all leads to some rather ridiculous dialogues between Liberals and Conservatives:

Liberal: *"We have to do something about hunger. Studies show that 25% of the children in this country go to bed hungry."*

Conservative: *"Oh, come on now. You know as well as I do that those studies are complete nonsense. All a person had to do was report that their child said, 'Mommy, I'm hungry,' just one time during a twelve-month period to be counted in the study as 'going to bed hungry.' What child hasn't said 'I'm hungry' more than once in the last year?"*

The gauntlet has been thrown. The Conservative has responded to the Liberal's charge with fact and some logic. Now, the last thing you are going to hear in this situation is the Liberal getting into a discussion about the methodology behind the study. That would involve facts and logic, not feelings and emotion. To save the day, the Liberal has to respond with more emotion:

Liberal: *"You're full of hate. You hate children. You want children to go off somewhere and die. You're evil. You don't care if children starve to death."*

If you think facts infuriate Liberals, you ought to see what logic does to them. Many Leftists have ended up in lengthy lethargic stupors as a result of having been exposed to toxic (to Liberals) doses of logic.

Let me give you an example.

I have used this analogy dozens of times in conversations with my liberal friends and listeners during discussions over welfare policy. Over the years I have personally witnessed three minds snap completely and six cases of excessive slobbering and drooling by Liberals trying to handle this question logically.

The underlying discussion is whether or not it is proper for the government to take money from one person by force and then simply give that money to another person (a welfare, food stamp, or Medicaid recipient, for example) for his personal use.

To begin the discussion, I bring up the point that our government, as our Constitution says, derives its powers "from the consent of the governed." The idea here is that we cannot and should not ask the government to do anything for us that we cannot legally or morally do for ourselves.

Sounds logical, doesn't it?

With that premise in mind, I build the following scenario:

You live in a triplex. You are in apartment No. 1, Johnson is in apartment No. 2, and Wilson lives in No. 3.

You discover that Wilson is ill and cannot work. He never bothered to buy a health insurance policy because he just didn't believe he would need it for quite some time. He has no savings because it was more important to spend his money on Bondo for his Camaro and a good Panama City Beach vacation every summer.

You believe that Wilson is about to starve to death. His electricity is going to be cut off and he can't afford to buy his blood pressure medication. You decide to help, charitable soul that you are. You scrounge through your bank account and find $200 to help your neighbor out.

Good for you. What a guy!

Wilson, though, is still in trouble. Your $200 wasn't enough. It turns out that he spent $20 for a case of beer and at least another hundred or so at the dog track. Things may not be all that desperate, though. One of the 35 Lotto tickets he bought with that carton of cigarettes might pan out.

You decide to go visit Johnson in apartment No. 2 to see if he can chip in. Johnson tells you that, while he certainly understands the seriousness of Wilson's situation, he needs his money to send his daughter to college in the fall and to pay some of his own medical bills. Besides, he's trying to save up some cash for a down payment on a house so he can get out of this weird apartment.

You determine that it is far more important for Wilson to have some of Johnson's money than it is for Johnson to keep it and spend it on his own needs. So, here's your question:

Do you, at that point, have the right to pull out a gun and point it right at the middle of Johnson's forehead? Can you demand that he hand over a few hundred dollars for Wilson's care, and tell him that you'll be back to get some more next month?

You won't find many people who will tell you that they have the right to take Johnson's money by force and give it to Wilson. They might say that they would try to talk Johnson into being a bit more charitable, but they won't say they have the right to rob him at gunpoint.

Then comes the killer question:

"Well, if our government derives its powers from the consent of the governed, how can you ask your government to do something for you that, if you did it for yourself, would be a crime?"

At this point you sit back and watch your liberal friend wrestle with his battle between compassion and logic. Logic will tell him that you have a definite point here. His compassion will tell him that it doesn't matter; hand over the money.

To the Liberal, Wilson's grave situation and his need for money supersedes any questions about the morality and legality of transferring income, by force, from Johnson to Wilson.

As pointed out earlier, Liberals also have a tendency to view people not as individuals but as members of groups. There are very few individual identities to Liberals, only group identities.

Again, all you have to do is sit back and listen. Liberals will talk of "the poor," "the less fortunate," "the Blacks," "the rich," "the disadvantaged," and so on. You just don't seem to have a meaningful existence to a Liberal if you can't be categorized into some group.

Conservatives, on the other hand, tend to consider people as individuals rather than as members of groups.

Not only do Liberals not think in terms of individuals, but the very word is offensive to many of them. Several years ago a young female student served on the Diversity Committee at a state university. This student became concerned that the deliberations of the Diversity Committee did not favor the rights of individuals on campus.

So she wrote a letter to the other members of the committee telling them of her concerns and of her abiding belief in the concept of individual rights.

The letter found its way to the faculty member advising the committee.

It was later returned to the offending student with several notations, including the word *individual* being outlined in red.

Alongside the offending word, the professor wrote a note telling the student that she should exercise restraint in her use of the word individual since many people consider it to be racist.

Racist? The word *individual* is racist? How in the world could that be?

The professor explained that any attention or recognition paid to individuals strengthens the concept of the individual over that of the group. Since the majority group in this country is white, the term *individual* strengthens the concept and image of the white individual over all others. This makes the term racist.

We immediately know a few things about this professor:

1. He's a bloomin' fool.
2. He's a Liberal (see No. 1).
3. He wouldn't have a prayer of finding meaningful employment in the private sector.
4. He can't define racism.

There are many other ways to differentiate between Liberals and Conservatives. Liberals, for instance, drive Volvos and wear glasses that are way too small for even *their* pointy heads.

Liberals like domestic animals that defecate in the

house. That's understandable, considering that's what they have been doing to our sense of independence for decades.

Liberals think that America is great because of its government. Conservatives think that America is great because of the incredible spirit and energy that comes from free people interacting freely with each other.

Liberals like to look to the government for solutions to any and all problems. In fact, they're quite insulted if you ever suggest that the government has no role in solving a particular problem. Conservatives look to individuals to solve their own problems, knowing that government solutions are always very expensive and almost never successful.

So. . . you may be wondering whether I am a Liberal or a Conservative.

Neither. I'm a Libertarian.

You aren't ready for that one yet.

DECISIONS. . .
Decisions

Barring extreme physical and mental disabilities, each and every one of us is where we are today — be it poor or wealthy, happy or sad, on the streets or in a condo, in a Mercedes or a rusted-out Pinto — because of the choices we have made during our lives.

It's the choices we have made that put us where we are, not the choices others have made for us.

This statement brings the mental lava boiling to the surface of many people. Imagine that you are 40 years old and still renting an apartment. You have a six-year-old car that isn't paid for, not one penny in a savings account, no retirement plan, you are starting your fourteenth job next Monday, and you are getting a bit weary of seeing your face on the "Deadbeat Dads" public service announcement on television.

Along comes some clown saying you are in that position because of the choices you have made during your life.

Like hell! It's not *your* fault that you can't keep a job. All of those people you were working for were just unreasonable in their demands. You couldn't control the traffic that made you late so many times. And it certainly wasn't *your* fault that your car kept breaking down. Lousy American cars.

Savings? Retirement? How in the world can you save anything, what with the price of a six-pack and all? Those greedy businessmen just won't pay you enough to allow you to save.

And what about that child support? That judge knew that you couldn't afford to pay that much money in child support! You have to live, too! Sure, you could have sent her *something* every month and she might have been satisfied, but she's just trying to ruin your life and you aren't going to fall for *that* again.

Those people out there with their own homes and their good jobs and fancy cars. . . they were just lucky! They got all the breaks. Nobody out there even wants to give me a chance.

Our whining little friend just can't — or won't — see reality.

Obviously he isn't educated well enough or doesn't have the job skills to get a good, high-paying job. If you could rewind a tape of his life and watch it on fast forward, you would see him making choice after choice that led to his failure to acquire an education. The choice to clown around in class rather than pay attention. The choice to watch television rather than do homework. The choice to play touch football with the other kids rather than study for that test. The grand overview will show that he chose not to become educated.

The poor choices kept mounting up. The choice not to leave home earlier so that traffic wouldn't make him late for work. The choice to spend money on a fishing trip instead of keeping his car in running condition. The choice to leave work early for a beer with the guys instead of staying a bit longer to wrap up some loose ends. The choice to turn down that after-hours training program that could have given him more job skills. Too much time away from the girlfriend.

And who can imagine the choices he made that got him into his child-support trouble? At the head of the list might be the choice to have children that he and his wife could not yet afford to raise. This led to financial hardships in the marriage (the No. 1 cause of divorce, by the way) and finally to his "Deadbeat Dad" picture on television.

So why does our sad friend get so outraged when I come yammering along with my admonition that his own choices put him where he is?

Simple. It's because he is being told that *he* is responsible for what has happened to him. *Him.* Not his boss, not his teachers, not his wife, not the children, not the judge. . . but *him.*

If you haven't already noticed it, you soon will — people will do anything, say anything, believe anything to escape accepting responsibility for their own lives.

One of the greatest signs of maturity in any individual are the words "It's my fault. I'm responsible. I made some really stupid decisions. But I'm not going to let it happen again." If you ever hear someone utter those words, hire him. Once you get about ten of them around, you can own the world.

Don't wait until it is too late to recognize the importance of good decision making. Human beings are the only creatures who have the ability to analyze several complicated courses of action and then choose the one that they think will best move them toward their goal. That's your gift. Don't waste it.

If you make the right choices, revel in them. Celebrate your success.

If you make poor choices, accept responsibility for them. Remember, there are always more choices to be made; and the right ones will move you further toward your own idea of success and happiness.

"THOSE LESS Fortunate"

There is one phrase that bothers me more than most. You have heard it, and will continue to hear it, time and time again. It rolls off the tongues of news anchors and reporters and out of the printers of columnists and editorialists with abandon.

"The less fortunate."

The phrase is used to refer to people who are not what you might, even in a moment of great charity, call "winners." We're talking about single women with children they can't afford to raise; fathers who abandon their children; high school dropouts with no job prospects; drug addicts and winos begging for money for their next hit; and various other easily recognizable losers.

These people, according to the media, are the "less

fortunate." A typical sentence in a news story might be, "Welfare reform will make life more difficult for the less fortunate," or some such sentiment.

When the media types describe the urban outdoorsmen,[1] winos, drug addicts, high school dropouts, and various other losers as "the less fortunate," they are implying[2] that those people who escaped this lifestyle and actually became productive citizens did so because they were "more fortunate."

In other words, they were just flat lucky.

Robert Reich, Clinton's former Secretary of Labor and one of his most liberal advisors, liked to refer to the top 20% of income earners in the United States as "the fortunate fifth."

Bring out those dictionaries. My *Webster's* defines *fortunate* as "deriving good from an unexpected place."

Think about it. Is there anything "unexpected" about deriving good from hard work? Is there anything "unexpected" about deriving good from living a life free of illegal

---

[1] "Urban outdoorsmen" is a phrase I prefer when referring to the so-called homeless. The phrase gives those poor souls the image of an adventurer. You don't take people living in the mountains of Colorado and describe them as "homeless," do you? Well, lets give the same respect to those living in the concrete canyons.

[2] Has anyone figured out the difference between imply and infer yet?

drugs and with only a moderate consumption of alcohol? Is there anything "unexpected" about deriving good from staying in school, not getting pregnant, developing marketable skills, and getting a job?

Hardly.

"Fortune" or "luck" has little to do with it. Luck, they say, is nothing less than opportunity met by preparation.

If you work hard, take advantage of the opportunities you have living in America, and keep your nose clean, you will succeed, and it won't be because you were fortunate or lucky. It will be because you made smart choices and worked hard.

How, then, do we account for the popularity of the "less fortunate" phrase when referring to people who, more often than not, have done nothing less than completely squander their American birthright?

Here's the logic.

Imagine that you are a modern big-government Liberal.[3] You believe that America is great because of its government, not because of its people. You want more

---

[3]For many of you just out of college, this will not be difficult. As you continue to work in the real world, this will become quite a challenge.

government programs and more spending. You are just brimming over with compassion[4] for the "less fortunate."

One of the things you, as a Liberal, really like about government is that government has the power to "level the playing field," so to speak, by redistributing income. You believe wholeheartedly in taking from the rich and giving to the poor. It is not enough to strive for equal opportunity. The true goal must be equality of results. A nice, well-ordered, egalitarian society.

Now, if it is your goal to take money away from people who worked hard and earned it, and then to give that money to people who did not earn it, you are going to need a convincing story, an excuse, a reason.

Well, how's this?

Those people with all the money got that way because they were lucky. They were just fortunate. It's not that they are any smarter or better than anyone else, or that they worked any harder. They were just fortunate. They were in the right place at the right time. They had the right skin color. They were lucky because they got to go to a better school.

---

[4]As you aldredy know, it is easy to show compassion with someone else's money.

And what about those people living on the streets or in the homeless shelters, or wasting away in a public housing project with babies they can't afford to raise? Well, those people aren't there because they are less intelligent, or because they didn't work as hard as the others. They just weren't lucky enough. They weren't fortunate enough. They didn't get the breaks everyone else gets. They are the "less fortunate."

So, now that you have convinced yourself (and others) that those people with money were just lucky, and those people without enough money were not as lucky, you find it easier to make a case for just taking money away from those lucky, fortunate folks and giving it to those poor unlucky, "less fortunate" folks.

After all, it's not like they actually went out there and worked for that money! They didn't sacrifice anything. They were just lucky. They were the "fortunate." All you're doing is just evening out the odds a bit. Gee, that would only be fair, wouldn't it?

One of my favorite big-government Liberals, Missouri democrat Richard Gephardt, reached all-time absurd levels in 1996 in playing up this "fortunate – not fortunate" idea that Liberals love so. He referred to those people in our society who enjoy high incomes as a result of hard work and good decision making as "those who won life's lottery."

Life's lottery?

If you stay in school, keep your nose clean, work hard and make responsible choices, and, as a result, become successful, you have won a lottery?

What a colossal insult!

You walk up to someone who has been working 60-hour weeks since the day he got out of school to become successful and suggest that his comfortable lifestyle is due to nothing more than the right ping-pong balls falling into the chute. Then duck.

The motive behind Gephardt's insulting "won life's lottery" remark is the same as for those who use the "less fortunate" phrase. If a person has all of that money because of luck or a lottery drawing, what's the big problem with making him share it? It's not as if he actually *worked* for it.

Learn this now: Life is not a lottery.

Nobody knows where the ping-pong balls will fall. Nobody knows when luck will strike. But every rational person knows the result of hard work and wise choices. The result is, in a word, success.

THE WORLD'S EASIEST
Sure-Fire Savings Plan

No, this book hasn't suddenly turned into a financial planning manual. But I am going to present you with the easiest savings plan ever devised. This plan has never failed with any person who actually gave it a fair try.

In the winter of 1987 I joined a group of Atlantans on a ski trip to Vail, Colorado. My roommate for the trip was a construction worker named Bill.

Our first night, while fortifying our bodies with drinks for the ravages of the slopes the next day, Bill explained how he saved money every year for this ski trip.

I adopted his savings plan and it has worked wonders for me. If you are just out of college and just starting out on your career, it can work wonders for you, too.

The plan is very easy and can be summed up in one four-word sentence: **Never spend dollar bills.**

When you leave your home for work in the morning, have absolutely no one-dollar bills in your pocket. Carry only fives, tens, or twenties. Carry fifties and hundreds if you got 'em, but don't lose your wallet or purse.

During the day, whenever you spend any money, take any one-dollar bills you might get in change and you put them in a separate pocket. Do not spend those bills.

If, for instance, you want a cup of coffee on the way to work, pay for it with a five-dollar bill. There will be three or four one-dollar bills in the change. Those bills get put away. Again, do not spend them. This means the cup of coffee is taking several dollars out of the cash you have available for spending that day. That's the idea! If you can't afford to set those dollar bills aside, then don't get the cup of coffee! Save that five-dollar bill for lunch.

Follow this same routine all day long. When you buy something, pay for it with either the change in your pocket or with any bill larger than a one. Take whatever dollar bills you get in change (usually not more than four) and set them aside.

When you get home at the end of the day, take all of the dollar bills you have gathered and you put them in a box or other safe place.

Wait until the end of the month to see how many of these dollar bills you have. I guarantee, you will be stunned.

I have talked to people who swore that they did not have one dollar to spare for savings. They just weren't making enough. They needed every single penny to pay rent, car payments, food, and some clothes. No way they could save.

I convinced them to try the dollar-bill scheme for just one month. At the end of that month, I have never had anyone tell me they saved less than one hundred dollars.

I have told the listeners to my radio show of this savings plan several times. Not one week goes by that I don't get a letter from one of them telling me how he saved for a car, a vacation, even a down payment for a house with this plan.

It works. All you have to do is try it for yourself to find out how well.

So, what is the lesson of this dollar-bill savings program?

There are several lessons. The first is that as you go through each day every choice you make, no matter how inconsequential it may seem, is important. Every time you make a decision to buy and to stick with your plan and put those dollar bills aside, you are exercising a choice. The impact of those seemingly small choices will be known to you at the end of the month when you count those dollars.

The other lesson has to do with debt. You will learn with this exercise that you can save large sums of money one dollar at a time.

There is another side to this coin. You can also get deeply into debt the same way — one dollar at a time.

Just as you have to make a decision on each and every dollar you spend, so, too, do you have to make decisions on each and every dollar you charge to that little credit grenade (card) you carry in your pocket. Just one dollar at a time. . . and before you know it, you are in debt up to your ears.

It's just as easy to go into debt as it is to save. The choice is yours.

By the way, you know that huge federal debt we have? You know, don't you, that the interest alone we pay on that national debt is the second largest item in our federal budget?

Well, we got into that debt situation — you guessed it — one dollar at a time. That's how we'll get out of it, too, if we ever do. Watching those small expenditures carefully, one dollar at a time.

DON'T READ
These Books

Maybe you read this book on a dare. Perhaps it was part of a work-release program, or you found it on the coffee table of a halfway house for recovering bedwetters. If your parents, or some other people who care about your current mental state, gave this to you after your graduation, you might have read it out of some misplaced sense of duty.

Whatever your reason for plowing this far, you've had enough. There is no sense in continuing this torture. You have been wearing the badge of a bona fide Liberal with pride. And so far, this unnerving exposure to the dark world of logic and fact has left you bruised and questioning your beliefs.

At this point, then, I urge you to be *very* careful about any other books that some of your so-called friends might try to push into your hands. It's enough that they gave you this one. Don't sit back and meekly allow this abuse to continue.

To help you feel safe and secure in your hyper-compassionate emotion-based existence, I have listed here several books which I strongly urge you not to read. These books could cause some rather severe intellectual discomfort, especially if you are suffering from a desire to single-handedly save humanity from itself, or if you have been diagnosed with Obsessive-Compulsive Compassion Disorder.

Avoid these books like the plague.[1]

ATLAS SHRUGGED.

This book, written by a Russian immigrant named Ayn Rand, is the big kahuna. Thankfully it is more than 1,000 pages long, which makes it unattractive to most Liberals who prefer fewer words, larger type, and more pictures.

You may be familiar with the classical image of Atlas struggling to balance the earth on his shoulders. He is stooped over, his legs are bent, and the strain is obvious on his face. Luckily, Atlas is strong and it appears that he can

---

[1] It is also a good idea to avoid clichés like the plaque.

hold on for quite a while.

What do you suppose might happen, though, if the weight of the globe on Atlas's shoulders kept increasing, getting heavier and heavier until it was almost unbearable? Not only is he bearing the increased weight of the world, but Atlas is just not getting enough respect. He is suffering insults and hatred from the very people he is holding up.

Finally, the burden gets to be a bit too much. One final straw, and Atlas shrugs.

Leave this book alone. There is a particularly dangerous speech from a character named John Galt, and the heroine smokes.

Besides, you don't want to devote the rest of your life looking for Galt's Gulch. After all, Galt's Gulch doesn't exist. . . or does it?

Sadly, *Atlas Shrugged* is available in most bookstores.

CAMP OF THE SAINTS.

Two good things about this book: First, it was written by a Frenchman named Jean Raspail. People aren't especially eager to read books written by Frenchmen. Second, the book is out of print. This means that it is really available only in libraries. I have personal agents in libraries all over the United States who keep this book constantly checked out so that it won't damage the mental health of our Leftist friends.

You've heard all of the arguments about immigration reform. Some people actually think that there is something a wee bit wrong about letting people come into this country and then telling the taxpayers that they must provide these newcomers with medical care, a place to live, food, and a nifty little cash income.

Well, *Camp of the Saints* is a pure wet dream to those who think we ought to change the Immigration and Naturalization Service into an International Welcome Wagon.

Imagine this: Every diseased, uneducated, unemployable, unsocialized, needy, pathetic person, along with their countless children, from every Third World country on this earth suddenly joins some sort of a mass exodus to the industrialized West.

Literally hundreds of millions of these impoverished people, along with their self-righteous leaders, manage to commandeer every boat that can still float in every obscure harbor of the world, and they all set sail for the coasts of America and Europe. The bodies of the dead are thrown over the sides as this armada makes its way. Their announced intention is to land on the shores of the wealthy countries of the world and demand their "right" to a share of the wealth — to be fed, clothed, sheltered, and cared for.

The great joy of this book is watching the professional do-gooders battle one another. They know disaster is on the way, but their grand sense of social responsibility just won't let them say no. Those with the gift of logical thought will love the depiction of the mental burn-out as the Liberals of the world shout, "My God! These people are coming to *my* door and they want *my* house and *my* money!"

It gets rich when tens of thousands of these rusted-out ships suddenly start anchoring a hundred yards or so off the coast of Europe and the United States. Not a pretty sight. And not a comfortable read for those still steeped in left-wing emotionalism.

If you do happen to see this book sitting on a library shelf, treat it like it was the personal journal of the last doctor who died trying to rid the world of the Ebola virus.

THE LAW.

The Law is now around 150 years old. To be exact, it was published as a pamphlet in June of 1850. Strangely enough, it's another book by a Frenchman — Frederic Bastiat. It is amazing that such wonderful (but dangerous) books can be written in such an incomprehensible, whiny language.

This is the book that turned me.

Yes, dear reader, remember that I, too, was once a dream-filled, holier-than-thou, super-compassionate Liberal. At Texas A&M I was in bed with Students for a Democratic Society. I spent countless hours moaning and grieving for the exploited, the oppressed, and the less fortunate.

Then I read *The Law*.

Bastiat wrote the book around the time of the French Revolution. Some powerful people back then were urging a socialist government and economy for France. Bastiat, an economist, thought that this wasn't such a great idea.

Bastiat wrote *The Law* in an effort to explain why socialism would be disastrous for France and why it simply would not work.

This book explains, better than any writing or any person ever has, before or since, just what the true purpose and function of government and the law are.

The Law is very short. It is short because it doesn't really take too many words to explain the role of the law in a free society. It takes many more words to explain the role of the law and government in a society that is not so free.[2]

If you are comfortable with your current liberal, big-government political positioning, don't read this book. It *will* change you. Avoid it at all costs.

The Law is not readily available in bookstores. It was published by some foundation way up north that promotes (gasp!) economic freedom. I could give you the name and address right here so that you could order it, but that might make it too likely that the book would end up in the hands of some comfortable Liberal.

So, if you don't know where to get *The Law* and you are intent on messing up your mind still further, tap into my home page on the Net. The address is << www.boortz.com >>.

OK. Now we have three books on this list — one by a Russian and two by Frenchmen. We need to get at least one American author on this list. So, after an extensive search, I found a book by an American author that will, if read by a doctrinaire Liberal, cause severe mental anguish, not to mention overload.

---

[2]Have you seen a copy of the Federal Registry lately?

THE WAY THINGS OUGHT TO BE.

This book is by Rush Limbaugh. Perhaps you've heard of him. He is our token American here. *All* talk show hosts owe Rush Limbaugh a debt of gratitude, whether they agree with him or not.

Rush Limbaugh has done for talk radio what Arnold Palmer did for golf. Before Arnie came along, many professional golfers had to give lessons to make ends meet. After Palmer, professional golfers needed weight training just to carry their wallets around.

Limbaugh's books are good, really! He shows excellent insight into just how we got ourselves into this mess and how we will get ourselves out.

QUICK Points!

Time now to make some quick points. There were only so many pages to fill before we reach the back cover, and I'm getting close. Each of these quick items could have been expanded to well over 1,000 words, but I'm not practicing law anymore,[1] so I don't get paid by the word. I just thought I would try out for the "Brevity Is the Soul of Wit" award.

WHY WE HATE THE RICH

One of the most powerful human emotions is envy. It is also one of the most easily manipulated emotions.

Politicians learned hundreds of years ago that people who had little material wealth were incredibly jealous of

---

[1]Thank you, God.

those who had more than they did. This deep-seated envy was ripe for exploitation — and the exploitation has been running rampant for generations.

There are far more voters in this country who do not consider themselves to be rich than there are voters who would claim that title. This means that politicians can slam the rich, damn the rich, tax the rich, roast the rich, and eat the rich without putting too many votes in jeopardy.

Note, please, the ways that Liberals love to refer to the rich. We have "filty rich," "ungodly rich," "robber barons," and many other titles that are somewhat less than complimentary.

This anti-wealth propaganda has had an effect. When you poll Americans about the wealthy, you will find that the majority of people feel that rich people came about their money in some dishonest manner. They had crooked lawyers. They cheated on their income taxes. They exploited others. They consumed more than their "fair share" of the world's resources, and so on.

There is a deep-seated psychological need for those who are not wealthy to assume that the wealthy got that way through evil and illegal means.

If you recognize that most wealthy people got that way

through hard work, the wise use of their power of choice, and the willingness to take risks, you are stuck with the problem of figuring out just why you're not up there with them. What's the matter? Don't you want to work hard? Are you afraid to take risks? Are you not willing to put time and thought into your decision-making process?

Naw. . . this isn't going to work. If you agree that the rich are good, then you have to develop excuses about why you're not wallowing in money.

But ... if you adopt the attitude that the rich are evil — that they used crooked lawyers to take advantage of innocent people, that they exploited their workers and ravaged the enviroment — you will find it easier to make excuses for your own lack of success.

After all, *you* aren't evil. *You* don't have a crooked lawyer. *You* don't exploit innocent workers or take advantage of innocent waifs, and you aren't an enemy of the environment.

That's why you aren't rich. It's because you are *good.* And those rich people are *bad.*

Wow! What a wonderful rationalization! It sure gets you off the hook, doesn't it? And it makes you a willing myrmidon to any politician who wants to exploit this mindset for his own personal gain.

SOUNDS SORT OF FAMILIAR

I have never been one to find Communists under every bed. Frankly, religious zealots have been more worrisome to me than Communists, even before the fall of the Soviet Union and the Berlin Wall. At least the Communists never tried to tell us that God gave them express permission to rule.

There has been one little phrase that, over the years, has been closely associated with communism and socialism. It appears in the Communist Manifesto. You've heard it before; now here it is in writing: "**From each according to his ability. To each according to his needs.**"

I have noticed a return of this little ditty during recent years. It seems to be on the minds of a lot of Liberals in the Clinton administration.

As soon as Clinton took office in 1993, he started pushing his retroactive tax increase on upper-income Americans. "The rich," he said, "need to pay their fair share."[2] When people asked him why he planned to raise taxes only on the wealthy and not across the board, he replied that he wanted

---

[2]You've already read in "Who Really Pays the Taxes" that the "rich" have been paying far more than their "fair share" for quite a while.

to hit the rich with a tax increase " . . . because that's where the money is."[3]

"From each according to his ability."

After the voter revolution of 1994, the Republicans took a majority position in Congress. They immediately started talking about tax cuts. As luck would have it, many of these tax cuts would benefit the rich.

The Clinton administration wasted no time at all in decrying the idea of allowing the rich to keep any more of the money they earn. Clinton's Labor Secretary, Robert Reich, said that such a tax cut was not warranted because the rich "don't need it."

"To each according to his needs."

Ah, but I'm probably just imagining things.

THE TRUTH ABOUT GUN CONTROL

We certainly aren't going to solve the gun control mess here, but there are a few things you need to think about as the debate rages on:

---

[3]As it turns out, Clinton's tax increase, which passed Congress by one vote, had its most damaging impact on the middle-income groups. So much for his campaign promise of a middle-class tax cut.

1. Those who favor gun control never seem to have any plan to take guns out of the hands of criminals. All the plans for gun registration, waiting periods, concealed-weapons laws and ownership bans affect only those people who obey the law. These aren't the people who are using guns to rob, rape, and murder.

   More than 90% of the guns used in crimes are obtained outside of regular commerce. This means that they aren't bought at gun stores and they aren't registered to the person who used them in the crime. This means that laws aimed at retail gun sales don't even begin to address the problem.

2. Guns don't kill people. People kill people with guns.

   I am both amused and outraged when I read headlines like "Gun Kills Three" or "Guns Responsible for Deaths." So far as I know, there has never been one single case where a gun has, on its own, decided that it would be a nifty idea to hop out of that nightstand drawer it has been trapped in and head on down to the local convenience store for a quick robbery.

   The gun control crowd likes to blame violence on the guns. That way they aren't actually breaking one of the most basic liberal rules: "You shall not hold an individual responsible for his actions."

3. In any given year about 99.98% of all of the privately owned handguns in the entire country *are not* used in a murder. About 99.6% of the privately owned handguns *are not* used in a crime of any description. Wow! This really shows the urgency for strong gun control, doesn't it?

Here's an idea: Why not concentrate on the small minority of people who are using guns for criminal purposes, rather than the vast majority who own their guns peacefully and at no risk to anyone who doesn't mean them harm?

YOUR INCOME TAX WITHHOLDING

Some day you may wonder why your income taxes are taken out of your paycheck before you ever even see the money. Why can't you just write a check for your income taxes the same way you do for your car payment and child support?

Because the government doesn't want a tax revolt, that's why.

You may be surprised to know that up until World War II that is exactly what American wage earners did. They took their entire paycheck home and wrote a check to the government every year for the taxes they owed.

During World War II the Political Class told us that they needed to speed up the cash flow a bit in order to pay for the war effort. No problem, the American people were in a mood to do anything it took. So the government started withholding taxes from paychecks before the wage earners ever saw them.

Here's the kicker: We were *promised* that as soon as the war ended the withholding would end, and we would go back to the old way of paying those taxes once a year.

In case you haven't noticed, the war is over. It's been over for quite some time now.

So, why is withholding still with us?

Very simple. In spite of the promises that were made, withholding is still with us because politicians know with absolute certainty that there would be an instantaneous and universal tax revolt if people actually had to pay their taxes by check.

Our Political Class could not continue the wild spending spree that keeps it in power if the Taxpayer Class had any idea at all just how much they are paying in taxes.

Oh, do you think that most people know anyway? It's

right there on their check stub, right?

Fair enough. You go ahead and believe that …right up until the next April 15 rolls around. Then give this little experiment a try.

Walk up to a couple of people in your office, or some friends, and ask them how much tax they had to pay this year. Remember, do this right around April 15 so that the vision of that tax return will still be sharp in their minds.

Ten to one you get this mindless response: "Oh, I didn't have to pay any! I'm getting some back!"

Of all the brain-dead, moronic things you will ever hear a human being say, this one takes the cake. This person doesn't even know how much he paid in taxes. He thinks the government is "giving" him something back!

Don't you know politicians just *love* this?

Carry it a bit further. Ask some of your friends what they make. Damned if some of them won't say, "I take home about $_____ a week."

"Take home? I didn't ask you how much you took home. I asked you how much you *made*!"

Our leaders have us thinking in terms of "take-home pay." We have been so blinded by this withholding non-sense that we don't even know how much money we are making anymore. We just know how much the Imperial Federal Government left for us to spend on ourselves.

THE MINIMUM WAGE

I just thought I would mention this one here, because it really frosts me big time!

I am sick to death of hearing Liberals talk about how difficult it is to raise a family on the minimum wage.

Why oh why doesn't someone walk up to one of these people and say, "Hey, pal, you're not *supposed* to raise a family on minimum wage. If you don't have the job skills or the wherewithal to earn more than the minimum wage, then you don't have any business having children, because you can't afford to raise them!"

One of the greatest social crimes a couple can commit is to have a baby that they cannot afford to raise.

THE RICH GET RICHER, AND THE POOR GET POORER

This one is so easy to explain. The rich keep getting richer because they keep doing the things that made them rich. Ditto for the poor. See how simple this all is?

4 8 Seconds

You're flying a small single-engine airplane on a nice VFR day. "VFR" stands for "Visual Flight Rules," which means you're not flying in or near to clouds and can see where you're going. You can look for other airplanes, and they can look for you, thus hopefully avoiding a chance, unhappy mid-air encounter. It's a typical hot and hazy summer day, but you can still see the ground and the horizon. You have a good feel for the "attitude" of the airplane: whether it is turning left or right, descending or climbing. With this type of visibility, you aren't going to inadvertently fly into the ground or the side of a mountain. The engine is purring and all is well with the world.

Suddenly you notice you can't see the horizon any more. The haze has become a bit thicker. A few seconds later you can't see the ground. All of the references you were depending on outside the windows of that airplane are suddenly gone! Even the tips of your wings seem to fade away into the haze!

You have flown into the clouds. This is what pilots call IMC, or "Instrument Meteorological Conditions." You, my friend, are flying on instruments. If you are a trained instrument pilot, no problem. If you're not, the statistics say you have 48 seconds to live. Maybe 50.

Up until this point in your flight you have been depending, in large part, on your visual references. You could look at the horizon and tell if your wings were level, not to mention which side of your airplane is up and which side is down. You could look at the ground, or directly ahead, to see if you were turning or flying straight. You might have glanced at your instrument panel every few seconds to see if you were holding your altitude, but, by and large, your eyes were outside of the airplane.

When you flew into the clouds, though, it became a different matter. Without those familiar visual references, it's only you and those dials and gauges on your instrument panel.

Suddenly your senses tell you that the airplane is turning! You can feel the movement. . . the left wing dips and you feel strange pressures against your seat. You take a quick look at the instrument panel but quickly discount what those instruments tell you. Your body and senses tell you one thing. Those gauges tell you another. You decide to trust your own senses. After all, they haven't failed you yet!

You have been in the clouds for about 15 seconds now. You have about 33 seconds left.

You're still fighting the definite feeling that the airplane is turning. You turn the yoke just a bit to the left. There! That feels better!

27 seconds.

You take another look at the instruments. Funny, they show you with your left wing down. That compass is turning, and the altimeter is moving. Now you're convinced that something must be wrong with those instruments. You twist the yoke just a bit more. . . there! That feels about right.

20 seconds.

Many miles away some air traffic controller is watching you on his radar screen. He can see that you are turning sharply to the left and losing altitude! He can't get you on the radio, though. You're too busy trying to fly the airplane, and, besides, you aren't on his radio frequency.

15 seconds.

You think you have everything under control. You should fly out of this cloud any moment now. As soon as you get on the ground you're going to sign up for those instrument flying lessons. You're not going to get caught like this again!

10 seconds.

Suddenly you do fly out of the cloud. Only it's the bottom of the cloud.

8 seconds.

Something's wrong! You're in a steep bank to the left and losing altitude quickly! The ground is spinning in your windshield!

5 seconds.

You yank back on the yoke! You have to stop this descent! The airplane shudders and the left wing drops some more!

3 seconds.

The airplane stalls and spins into the ground.

0 seconds.

Time's up, and you've just been given the celestial pink slip. In a few hours the inspectors from the National Transportation Safety Board are going to be picking over the wreckage of your aircraft trying to figure out just how and why you died.

The answer is always the same. Incapable of interpreting and trusting the instruments, the untrained pilot will instead rely on his own senses or intuition. . . and eventually come spinning out of the bottom of the cloud to his death.

A pilot in that situation needs to put his full faith in something completely outside of his own senses. That's where those instruments on the panel of his airplane come into play. They tell him where he is. What his airplane is doing. And just what he needs to do to stay alive and find his way back to clear skies. The pilot's body and "feelings" are going to tell him that those instruments are wrong. Actually, it's stronger than that. The pilot's body is going to insist that those instruments are wrong. If he believes and trusts in his body and senses, he dies. If puts his faith in those instruments, he survives.

Your journey through the remainder of your life is going to be much like that pilot's trip.

We, like many pilots, are fortunate that we spend most of our personal lives flying VFR. Our visibility is reasonably clear. We can see our goals, as well as the obstacles that stand in our way. We usually know in what direction we are heading, and we can tell whether or not we are making good speed. We can see the horizon, and that helps us keep our "wings" level. All is well in our little corner of the world.

Then we fly into a cloud.

The truth is that it is extremely unlikely you are going to complete life's journey without encountering some IMC. Sooner or later we all fly into rough weather. For some of us the trip is short. Others have a long way to go before they can see the horizon again.

When you hit the "soup" (and eventually you will), if you try to rely on your senses, on your "feel," on your intellect and intuition to get you back into the clear weather, you stand a good chance of becoming another 48-second statistic.

Just as with that pilot who flew into the clouds, we need instruments that we can refer to and put our absolute faith in when we go from the sunshine to the rain. We need instruments... something... that will give us unerring guidance back into the clear weather where we can once again rely on our vision and our senses to continue our journey.

I'm talking about *faith*.

If the pilot in the clouds puts his faith in those

instruments, he will live to see the numbers at the end of that runway. If you find something to put your faith in during times of trouble and stress, during the times you are in the clouds, you will survive to see happier times.

It is not my intent to preach religion here. There are other writers who are much better at that than I. I am merely suggesting that a core belief in something that surpasses your intellect, your "feel," or your "senses," will serve you well in troubling times.

Occasionally we really do get too smart for our own good. You've just completed four or more years of college. Your intellectual capabilities are at a peak right now. The brain is in overdrive, and you're ready to take on all challengers. This could be a dangerous time for you because you may truly think that you "know it all."

But nobody can ever know it all.

You are going to need some instruments to turn to when you can't see the ground.

For some, those instruments can be found in the Bible. For others, it might be the Koran or the Torah. You probably already have a sense of where your own set of instruments lies, but this new sense of intellectual dominance you bring out of college may have dulled your faith.

Right now you might think that your body and mind are better guides out of the darkness. Follow that hunch and start counting your 48 seconds.

Have faith in your instruments. Practice flying on those instruments until it becomes second nature to you. Practice until you can make that transition from sunshine to clouds and back again with ease.

Practice and keep practicing. Believe and keep believing. When all of your senses tell you that the instruments are wrong, have faith — and happy landings!